Other Schiffer Books by Elisabeth Bangert
Creative Ideas for Garnish & Decoration, 978-0-7643-3645-4, $19.99

Other Schiffer Books on Related Subjects:
Food Presentation: Tips & Inspiration, 978-0-7643-3481-8, $24.99
Food Art: Garnishing Made Easy, 0-7643-1960-4, $19.95
Herbs and Spices of the World, 0-916838-84-6, $45.00

Library of Congress Control Number: 2010931147

Type set in Linotype Finnegan (OFT)

ISBN: 978-0-7643-3648-5
Printed in China

Licensed by Edition XXL GmbH, Fraenkish-Crumbach 2009 www.edition-xxl.de

Concept and direction: Sonja Sammueller
Layout, setup and cover design: Sammueller Kreativ GmbH

Translated from the German by Dr. Edward Force

Published by Schiffer Publishing Ltd.
4880 Lower Valley Road
Atglen, PA 19310
Phone: (610) 593-1777; Fax: (610) 593-2002
E-mail: Info@schifferbooks.com

In Europe, Schiffer books are distributed by
Bushwood Books
6 Marksbury Ave.
Kew Gardens
Surrey TW9 4JF England
Phone: 44 (0) 20 8392 8585; Fax: 44 (0) 20 8392 9876
E-mail: info@bushwoodbooks.co.uk
Website: www.bushwoodbooks.co.uk

Contents

Asparagus

Scientists suspect that the tasty vegetable spikes originated in western Asia. In Egypt, asparagus was already being eaten about 5,000 years ago. The Greeks and Romans also got excited about asparagus plants. To the Greeks, it was a means of healing and magic. The Romans cultivated the plants and grew asparagus in gardens. Today it is grown around the world in regions with moderate to warm climates.

Three hundred years ago the green asparagus was the only known kind. Just about a century ago did man begin to raise white asparagus. Besides the white asparagus, the green and violet varieties also enjoy growing popularity.

Various Kinds to Choose

While the average person can differentiate between the pale and green types of asparagus, the consumer, to be sure, is less oriented to the various kinds than to the color and freshness.

1. White Asparagus

- It's milder in flavor than green asparagus
- It's cut before it comes into contact with sunlight.

2. Green Asparagus

- It's slightly reminiscent of young peas in flavor.
- It's less expensive and has more vitamins than white asparagus.
- Since it is grown on flat fields, it is easier to harvest than white asparagus.

3. Violet Asparagus

- It's cut only when the head comes out of the ground.
- It has a more expressive flavor.

4. Purple Asparagus

- It has an herb-like flavor.
- It grows above the ground.
- It's a special variety of green asparagus, but with a higher sugar content than the other kinds.

5. Wild Asparagus

- It comes from the Mediterranean area and tastes somewhat more tart and herb-like than green asparagus.
- It has thin spikes and almost grape-like heads.

Growing and Harvesting

The asparagus season begins, depending on the climate, in mid-April and ends on June 24. So that the tasty spikes reach our table crisp and fresh, most asparagus growers harvest twice a day: early in the morning and late in the afternoon; in optimal warm, moist weather, the tasty spikes grow up to 2 3/4 inches per day.

All kinds of asparagus must be harvested singly by hand even today. The practiced eye of the harvester recognizes the emerging asparagus by the cracks in the earth's surface and then digs it out with his fingers. With a special long asparagus knife, the spikes are then cut off above the rootstock. This must be done quickly—before the daylight discolors the noble vegetable. The "stabbed" asparagus is laid in baskets and covered to protect it from drying out.

Green asparagus is grown without asparagus walls and harvested when it has reached a length of about eight inches. It thrives even in heavy, porous soil in warm climates. It is sensitive to temperature changes, and in cold weather the green color can be delayed. The stalks are somewhat thinner than those of white asparagus, but very aromatic and heartier in flavor.

Asparagus in the Kitchen

Storage:

Unpeeled white asparagus stays fresh about two to three days, whereas peeled asparagus should be consumed after one day. The prerequisite for this durability is that it is wrapped in a damp cloth and stored in the vegetable drawer of a refrigerator. Green asparagus keeps growing after being picked, so it should be placed in water until it is used. The asparagus must never be exposed to frost, for that could cause damage from the coldness.

Preparation:

To keep asparagus from tasting woody, you should always peel white asparagus well and cut off the woody stalk ends generously. For wild and green asparagus, peel only the lower third and cut off the woody ends.

Buying:

When buying asparagus, you will be able to recognize its freshness best from the cut places. They should look smooth, light, and as juicy as possible. Fresh white asparagus "squeaks" when the stalks are rubbed on each other.

Trade Classes:

Asparagus is divided into various grades that assures its quality and makes shopping easier: Extra, First, Second, and Third Class are all suitable for eating asparagus; they differ only in diameter, shape, and coloring. However, the lower the trade class is, the more that should be removed when peeling.
Broken asparagus is suitable for soup or broth. It is usually very low-priced, can be purchased directly from the grower, and does not have to be rated by trade class.

Freezing Asparagus

Asparagus can be frozen splendidly! First blanch the peeled asparagus briefly.

For 1 1/8 pounds of asparagus, bring 8 1/2 cups of water to a boil after adding some lemon juice. Put the asparagus in and blanch for 3 minutes (only 1 1/2 minutes for green asparagus). Take it out of the water and cool it quickly in a bowl of ice water.
Now pat the asparagus stalks dry and place them on a kitchen shelf in the freezer. After it freezes, pack the asparagus in portions and store in the freezer.

If need be, simply place the frozen stalks in the cooking water without defrosting them, and prepare them as usual. You can freeze raw asparagus up to three months. When blanched, it remains tasty up to 10 months.
Pieces of asparagus do not need to be pre-frozen. They go directly into the package with some asparagus water and then into the freezer.

Traditional Preparation of Asparagus

*NOTE: Recipe is for four servings

4 1/2 lbs. asparagus · 1 pinch salt · 1-2 teaspoons sugar · 1 tablespoon butter · 2 tablespoons lemon juice (only for white asparagus!)

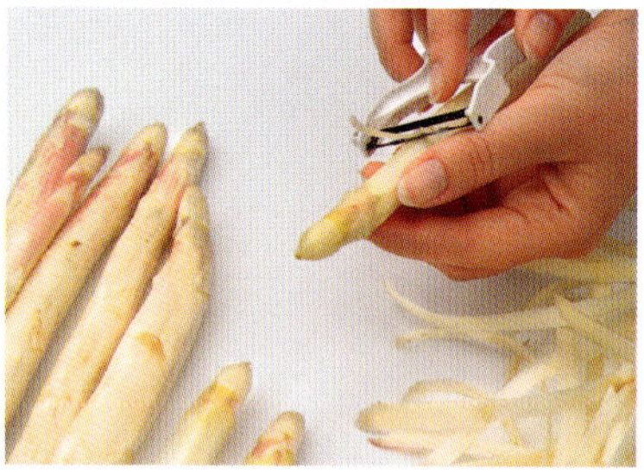

1. Wash the asparagus. Then, placing one at a time on your flat hand and beginning under the head, peel to the end.

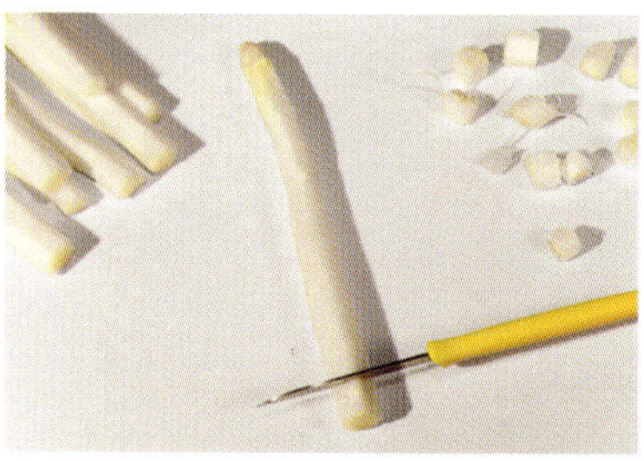

2. Now take the asparagus into your hand (the head should be pointing toward you) and, with a sharp knife, cut off the butt and remove the rest of the strings. The cutting place must be soft, so the asparagus won't be woody.

3. Put the peeled asparagus in the sieve liner of the asparagus pot. Fill the pot about 2/3 with water and boil. Add salt, sugar, and butter. Now and then asparagus can contain bitter substances, so a little sugar is added to the cooking water to neutralize this flavor somewhat. Put the sieve liner into the pot.

The cooking time will depend on the thickness of the asparagus stalks. The average is 10 to 15 minutes. Green asparagus stalks are usually thinner and, thus, will need less cooking time, about 8 to 12 minutes.
Lemon juice in the cooking water provides the gleaming white color of the tender stalks. The effect is wanted for the white type, but for the green, the juice should be left out, since a "bleaching effect" is not wanted.
The asparagus should still be somewhat chewy. Asparagus that has been cooked too long becomes watery and tasteless. By the way, the typical asparagus flavor is scarcely present if eaten raw. The tasty aroma develops only from warming it.
Thus it becomes completely "done" and tasty …

Asparagus Broth

Never throw the peels and cutoff ends away. Instead, use them to make a broth for soups or sauces.

1. Wash the peelings and cut-off ends of the asparagus stalks and let them dry.

2. Put the "asparagus junk" in a pot with water and some margarine. Bring to a boil and simmer on low heat about 10 minutes. Note: The broth can become bitter if cooked too long!

3. Drain everything through a sieve into a bowl in order to preserve as much of the contents that are directly under the skin, plus a lot of the flavor. Now you have the basis for aromatic sauces or creamy soup

NOTE: If you do not have an asparagus pot, you can naturally use a normal pot. Here a wide pot with a diameter of about 10 inches is suitable, as the asparagus can be cooked lying down and does not break.

Using Aluminum Foil or Roasting Sleeve

A water bath in the pot is not the only way to cook asparagus. The noble vegetable will also become nice and tender when cooked very gently in a roasting sleeve or with aluminum foil in a greased pan. How? Very simply!

Aluminum Foil

The silvery kitchen classic from the roll not only keeps foods fresh, but also is suitable for steaming meat, fish, or vegetables. In the process—from being wrapped in or covered with foil—the aroma and the nutrients are retained very well. New types of aluminum foil can even shorten the roasting time up to 30 percent.
Now, preheat the oven to 400°F and follow the cooking steps below.

1. Wash and peel the asparagus, cut off the woody ends, and lay out evenly in a greased pan or casserole dish.

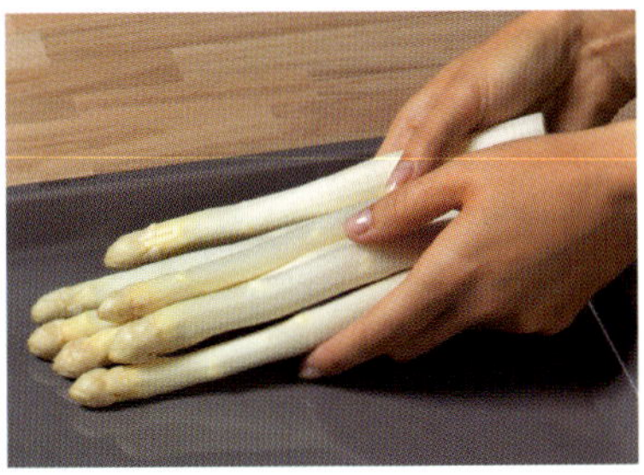

2. Dissolve seasoning salt and sugar in the water and pour over the asparagus. Scatter pieces of butter on top.

3. Cover the pan or dish with aluminum foil and bake in the oven for 50 to 60 minutes.

Roasting Sleeve

It's not only for fresh meat, poultry, and fish, but also crisp vegetables can be cooked quickly and simply in the roasting sleeve. The aroma, nutrients, and vitamins are largely retained in this protective cooking procedure while almost completely leaving out the addition of fat or oil.
Following the steps below, you can cook asparagus this simply in a roasting sleeve:

1. Cut the roasting sleeve to length (about 8 inches longer than the asparagus stalks) and close one end of it.

2. Now put the asparagus into the sleeve with some asparagus broth.

3. Close the other end of the sleeve and put it on the baking sheet with the sweat-seam upward. So that steam can escape, cut into the roasting sleeve about 3/8 inch at the seam before putting it in the oven (lowest level).

4. Now heat the oven to 350°F. Important: The foil must not touch the inside of the oven!

5. When it's done cooking, pull the pan out of the oven and carefully cut the inflated sleeve open.

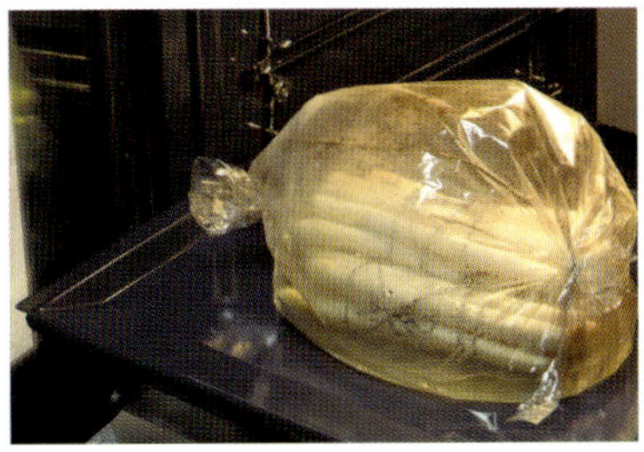

Making the Hollandaise Sauce

10 1/2 tablespoons butter · 2 fresh egg yolks · 1/4 cup white wine · 1 dash lemon juice · 1 pinch salt/pepper

1. Melt the butter in a small pot at low heat.

2. Boil some water in a pot.

3. Stir the egg yolks and white wine well in a metal bowl with a whisk. Put the bowl over the water bath and beat to a creamy, airy mass in about 3 minutes. Note: The material must not get too hot from the steam, or the egg will run!

4. Slowly add the melted butter, stirring constantly.

5. When the desired consistency is attained, flavor with lemon juice, salt, and pepper.

6. Serve the lukewarm sauce immediately!

The *Asparagus* Diet

Length of the diet: 5 days
Average daily calorie intake: 1,190 calories

Asparagus is good for the slim figure, as it contains all of 20 calories per 100 grams. Asparagus is also very healthy. It contains 1.5 percent fiber, helping to promote digestion, and is rich in the important vitamins B1, B2, C, and E. Plus, it contains the minerals potassium, phosphorus, magnesium, and iron. For spring tonics, asparagus is ideal — its high potassium content helps the body to get rid of water quickly and effectively, so the pounds disappear in no time!

In addition to the drinks featured in the diet plan, you should drink a lot of fluid: at least 2 liters a day. It is best to choose calorie-free drinks such as tea or mineral water. Drinks sweetened with sugar are hidden calorie bombs and should be avoided during diets. Dinkula is a German, sour-milk enzyme drink made from organic, whole meal spelt flour. It promotes digestion and strengthens the immune system. Dinkula can be purchased from health food distributors in Germany.

Diet Evaluation

Weight Loss	*****
Satiation	*****
Nutrition	***
Digestion	***
Practicality	*****
Convenience	**
Cost	**

DAY ONE

Total: 1,199 calories, 68.1 grams protein, 42 grams fat, 123.5 grams carbohydrate

Breakfast:

Fit-Maker Breakfast

322 calories, 17.6 grams protein, 2.8 grams fat, 55.4 grams carbohydrate

- 1 whole-grain (or rye) roll
- 1/4 cup cottage cheese
- 1 tablespoon low-fat yogurt
- 1 tomato
- Onion cubes
- 1/4 bunch parsley
- Salt and pepper
- 2/3 cup vegetable juice
- 1/2 cup Dinkula

Cut the roll in half, stir the cottage cheese and yogurt to a cream, and spread on the roll. Put tomato slices and onion cubes on one half, parsley on the other. Salt and pepper lightly. Stir vegetable juice with Dinkula and flavor to taste. Serve with the breakfast.

Snack:

Asparagus Salad with Strawberr

93 calories, 6 grams protein, 2.4 grams fat, 10.3 grams carbohydrate

- 1/2 lb asparagus
- 2/3 cup strawberries
- 3 1/4 tablespoons low-fat yogurt
- Lemon juice
- Pepper

Prepare bite-size pieces of asparagus as descr in Chapter One. Wash the strawberries and cu half. Flavor yogurt with pepper and lemon juic fold in asparagus and strawberries.

Lunch:

Asparagus with Salmon

429 calories, 32.1 grams protein, 20.7 grams fat, 27.1 grams carbohydrate

- 3 small potatoes
- 1 lb asparagus
- 2 teaspoons cooking oil
- 1/3 lb salmon fillet
- Salt and pepper
- 2 tablespoons low-fat yogurt
- Parsley, dill, and cress
- 3/4 cup Dinkula

Wash and peel potatoes and cook about 20 minutes in salt water. Wash the salmon fillet under cold running water, pat dry, salt, and pepper. Fry about 4 to 5 minutes on both side in hot cooking oil in a coated pan. Prepare asparagus as described in Chapter One. Put half of the asparagus in the refrigerator for dinner and the other half on a plate with the salmon and potatoes. Stir finely chopped herbs into yogurt, season with salt and pepper, and serve Serve Dinkula with it.

Energy Snack

118 calories, 1.4 grams protein, 0.3 gram fat, 26.8 grams carbohydrate

1 banana · 3/4 cup Dinkula · Mineral water

Mix Dinkula with mineral water and drink while eating the banana.

Dinner:

Asparagus Omelet

237 calories, 11 grams protein, 15.8 grams fat, 3.9 grams carbohydrate

- 16 spears cooked asparagus
- 2 eggs
- 2 tablespoons finely chopped herbs
- 1 pinch sea salt
- 1 teaspoon butter

Warm the asparagus briefly over steamed water. Meanwhile, beat the eggs well with 2 tablespoons of water and the herbs. Salt lightly. Heat the butter in a coated pan, mix the eggs in, and let it harden. Serve with the asparagus.

DAY TWO

Total: 1,197 calories, 92.2 grams protein, 32.3 grams fat, and 126.5 grams carbohydrate

Breakfast:

Wellness Bread with Strawberries

276 calories, 19.3 grams protein, 4.1 grams fat, 38.3 grams carbohydrate

- 2 slices whole-grain bread
- 1/2 cup cottage cheese
- 2/3 cup strawberries (sliced)
- 2 cups fasting tea

Spread cottage cheese on the bread. Wash the strawberries, cut them into slices, and put them on the bread. Drink fasting tea while you eat.

Snack:

Fiber Drink

125 calories, 6.3 grams protein, 2.5 grams fat, 18.6 grams carbohydrate

- 1/2 cup low-fat milk
- 1/2 cup French carrot juice
- 1/2 cup Dinkula
- 1 tablespoon soft oat flakes
- 1 tablespoon wheat bran

Stir the carrot juice, Dinkula, oat flakes, and bran into the milk and drink.

Lunch:

Sausage with Chicken

384 calories, 46 grams protein, 19.2 grams fat, 5.8 grams carbohydrate

- 1 lb asparagus
- 1/3 lb chicken breast
- 2 teaspoons olive oil
- 1 hard-boiled egg
- 3 tablespoons low-fat yogurt
- Paprika, salt, pepper, and fresh dill
- 3/4 cup Dinkula

Prepare asparagus as described in Chapter One. Meanwhile, wash the chicken breast under cold running water, pat dry, salt, and pepper. Heat oil in a coated pan and fry the chicken crispy brown all around. Remove the egg from its shell and cut it up fine. Cut the chicken breast into diagonal slices and put on the plate with 10 ounces of asparagus. Sprinkle with cut-up egg and garnish with dill. Also, serve yogurt dipped with dill and paprika. Drink Dinkula.

Snack:

Asparagus Salad with Crab

136 calories, 15.5 grams protein, 2.9 grams fat, 11.2 grams carbohydrate

- 1/2 lb asparagus
- 1/3 cup crab meat
- 1 tablespoon lemon juice
- 3 1/4 tablespoons low-fat yogurt
- 1 tablespoon finely chopped herbs
- Salt, pepper, and dill
- 1 slice crisp bread

Prepare asparagus in bite-size chunks as described in Chapter One. Drip some lemon juice on the crab and add to the asparagus. Stir yogurt into the herbs, flavor with lemon juice, pepper, and salt, and fold into the lettuce. Decorate with sprigs of dill and serve with the crisp bread.

Dinner:

Fruit Salad "Africana"

276 calories, 5.1 grams protein, 3.9 grams fat, 52.6 grams carbohydrate

- 1 small banana
- 1 kiwi fruit
- 1/2 papaya
- 3/4 mango
- 1 small orange and strawberries
- several lychee nuts
- gooseberries
- 1/2 teaspoon chopped pistachio nut
- 2 cups fasting tea

Peel the fruits, cut the banana and kiwi into slices, the mango into strips, and the papaya into bite-size chunks. Fillet the orange, shell the lychee nuts and remove the pits, slice the large strawberries, and remove the leaves from the gooseberries and wash them. Arrange the fruits on a plate and sprinkle with chopped pistachio nuts. Drink fasting tea with the salad.

DAY THREE

Total: 1,183 calories, 83.8 grams protein, 31.4 grams fat, 139 grams carbohydrate

Breakfast:

Vitamin Breakfast

319 calories, 4.3 grams protein, 1.2 grams fat, 74 grams carbohydrate

- 1/2 papaya
- 3 small bananas
- 1 1/4 cups watermelon (balled)
- 2 slices pineapple
- 3/4 cup Dinkula

Cut the papaya in half lengthwise, remove the seeds, and cut the fruit into thin strips. Use a scoop to make balls of the melon pulp and cut the bananas in slices. Arrange the fruit on a large plate and drink Dinkula with it.

Snack:

Tomato Drink

116 calories, 5.3 grams protein, 0.4 gram fat, 21.3 grams carbohydrate

- 2/3 cup tomato juice
- 1/2 cup Dinkula
- White pepper
- Chives
- 1 slice pumpernickel

Mix the tomato juice and Dinkula, flavor with pepper, and stir in pieces of chives. Serve well-cooled and eat a slice of pumpernickel with it.

Lunch:

Turkey Breast with Asparagus

290 calories, 37.5 grams protein, 9.1 grams fat, 13.5 grams carbohydrate

- 1 lb asparagus
- 1/3 lb turkey breast
- 2 teaspoons butter
- 1 cup strawberries (halved)
- 3 tablespoons low-fat yogurt
- 1 teaspoon lemon juice
- Sea salt, pepper, and curry powder

Prepare asparagus as described in Chapter One. Wash the turkey under cold running water, pat dry, and season with pepper. Heat butter in a coated pan and fry the turkey in it on both sides, then salt it lightly. Wash the strawberries and cut them in half. Cut half of the asparagus into bite-size chunks and save the rest for a snack. Cut the turkey breast into cubes. Prepare a dressing of yogurt and lemon juice; flavor with salt, pepper, and curry powder. Fold in the turkey breast and strawberries and let it warm briefly.

Snack:

Ham Rolls with Asparagus

138 calories, 13.7 grams protein, 1.7 grams fat, 17 grams carbohydrate

- 13 spears cooked asparagus
- 4 slices smoked ham
- 1 sprig of dill
- 1 slice pumpernickel

Roll the asparagus in very thin slices of smoked ham and decorate with the dill. Eat the slice of pumpernickel with it.

Dinner:

Green Asparagus with Mozzarella

320 calories, 23 grams protein, 19 grams fat, 13.2 grams carbohydrate

- 2/3 lb green asparagus
- 1/2 cup milk
- 1 egg yolk
- 1 teaspoon cornstarch
- 1/2 cup mozzarella (cubed)
- Salt, nutmeg, and lemon juice
- Chopped chervil
- 1 tablespoon finely cubed tomato

Prepare the asparagus as described in Chapter One. Stir the milk, egg yolk, and cornstarch together to make the sauce and bring to a boil while stirring. Cube the mozzarella, dissolving it in the milk. Flavor the sauce with the herbs and add the greater part of the chervil. Pour it over the asparagus and bake for 5 minutes in an oven preheated to 350-400°F. Scatter the tomato cubes and chervil leaves on it and serve.

DAY FOUR

Total: 1,165 calories, 59.1 grams protein, 31.4 grams fat, 159.5 grams carbohydrate

Breakfast:

Happy Breakfast

318 calories, 13.3 grams protein, 4.5 grams fat, 55.7 grams carbohydrate

- 2 slices crispbread
- 1/4 cup cottage cheese
- 1 tablespoon honey
- 3/4 cup low-fat milk
- 5 tablespoons orange nectar

Spread the cottage cheese on the crisp bread and put the honey on it. Mix the orange nectar with the milk and serve well-chilled.

Snack:

Orange Drink

112 calories, 7.4 grams protein, 1 gram fat, 17.3 grams carbohydrate

- 3/4 cup buttermilk
- 4 tablespoons orange nectar
- 1 teaspoon wheat bran

Mix the buttermilk with the orange nectar and the wheat bran, then drink.

Lunch:

Colorful Spring Salad

284 calories, 14.1 grams protein,
11.1 grams fat, 29.2 grams carbohydrate

- 1/2 lb asparagus
- 1 portion iceberg lettuce
- 1/2 small onion and 1 pearl onion
- 1/8 cup yellow pepper (strips)
- Several radishes
- 1 cup sour cream
- Salt and pepper
- Paprika powder and lemon juice
- 1 slice of bread
- 3/4 cup Dinkula

Prepare the asparagus as described in Chapter One. Meanwhile, clean and wash the lettuce and cut into bite-size chunks. Cut and pearl onion into slices, pepper into strips, and mix the salad ingredients with the asparagus. Mix the sour cream to a creamy state, season it with salt, pepper, paprika, and lemon juice, and use as salad dip. Add a slice of bread and drink Dinkula with it.

Snack:

Crispbread with Banana

156 calories, 2.5 grams protein,
1.7 grams fat, 32.6 grams carbohydrate

- 1 slice sesame crispbread
- 1 teaspoon reduced-fat butter
- 1 small banana

Spread the crispbread with the butter. Cut the banana lengthwise and place the slices on the bread.

Dinner:

Stuffed Eggs with Ham

295 calories, 21.8 grams protein,
13.1 grams fat, 24.7 grams carbohydrate

- 1 hard-boiled egg
- Several slices smoked ham
- 1 tablespoon sour cream
- 1 tablespoon low-fat yogurt
- 1 slice pumpernickel
- 3/4 cup Dinkula

Cut the egg in half, take out the yolk with a spoon, and mix with the sour cream and yogurt. Fill the mixture back into the egg halves with a piping bag. Serve with the smoked ham slices and pumpernickel. Drink Dinkula with it.

DAY FIVE

Total: 1,198 calories, 71.4 grams protein,
13.1 grams fat, 24.7 grams carbohydrate

Breakfast:

Exotic Muesli Cereal

303 calories, 10.8 grams protein,
5.9 grams fat, 49.8 grams carbohydrate

- 1/3 cup whole-grain fruit muesli
- 1/3 cup corn flakes
- 1 tablespoon oatmeal
- 1 kiwi fruit
- 1/4 mango
- 1 ounce gooseberries
- 1/2 cup low-fat yogurt
- Lemon juice
- 3/4 cup Dinkula

Mix the corn flakes and oatmeal with the muesli, peel the kiwi and cut into slices, and peel the mango, removing the core and cutting into pieces. Remove the leaves from the gooseberries, wash, and cut them in half. Flavor the yogurt with lemon juice and mix into the muesli. Drink Dinkula with it.

Snack:

Fitness Special

100 calories, 6.8 grams protein,
0.9 gram fat, 15.7 grams carbohydrate

- 2/3 cup buttermilk
- 2 tablespoons orange nectar
- 1 tablespoon soft oatmeal

Mix the buttermilk well with Dinkula, orange nectar, and the oatmeal, then drink.

Lunch:

Asparagus with Ham and Dip

314 calories, 18.0 grams protein,
23.9 grams fat, 5.5 grams carbohydrate

- 1 lb asparagus
- 1 hard-boiled egg
- 1 ounce thin raw ham
- 1/2 clove garlic
- 2/3 cup sour cream
- 1 tablespoon finely chopped herbs
- Salt, pepper, and parsley

Prepare the asparagus as described in Chapter One. Remove the egg from the shell and cut into fine pieces. Let the asparagus drain. Put half of it aside cold for dinner and arrange the rest of the asparagus on a plate with the ham and chopped egg. Decorate with parsley. Peel the garlic clove, squeeze, and mix into the sour cream. Add herbs, flavor with salt and pepper, and serve the dip with the asparagus.

Snack:

Fruited Crispbread

141 calories, 8.2 grams protein,
2.5 grams fat, 21 grams carbohydrate

- 1 slice crispbread
- 1/4 cup cottage cheese
- 1 small apple

Spread the crispbread with cottage cheese. Wash the apple, cut in half and remove the core, and slice into thin strips. Put some of the apple slices on the bread and eat the rest of the apple along with it.

Dinner:

Asparagus with Salmon

340 calories, 27.6 grams protein,
15.3 grams fat, 22.6 grams carbohydrate

- 13 spears cooked asparagus
- 1/4 lb smoked salmon
- Sprigs of dill
- 1 slice rye bread

Arrange the asparagus on a plate with the smoked salmon and decorate with dill sprigs. Eat the slice of rye bread with it.

Allgäutaler
zott
200g e

Asparagus Ham Rolls

- 24 spears of white asparagus
- 1 pinch of salt
- 1-2 teaspoons sugar
- 1 tablespoon butter
- 2 tablespoons lemon juice
- 7 slices of swiss cheese
- 8 slices of cooked ham (do not cut too thin)
- Some fresh parsley

Preparation:

1. Preheat oven to 350°F.

2. Wash the asparagus, peel it, and cut off the woody ends. Boil water with salt, sugar, butter, and lemon juice and then cook the asparagus in it for 10 to 15 minutes, depending on its thickness. Take it out and let it dry well.

3. Cut the cheese into 16 strips, and cut the ham slices into rectangles based on their shape. Wash the parsley, shake dry, and chop finely.

4. Wrap every three stalks of asparagus in a ham slice and encircle them with a strip of cheese.

5. Bake the rolls in the oven for a few minutes, until the cheese melts. Serve sprinkled with the chopped parsley.

NOTE: Unless otherwise noted, all of the recipes contained in this chapter are based on a serving of four.

Asparagus Soup

- 1 lb each white and green asparagus
- 1 pinch salt
- 1-2 teaspoons sugar
- 2 ounces butter
- 3/8 cup flour
- 3 teaspoons instant vegetable broth
- 1/2 glass white wine
- 1 2/3 cups crème fraîche
- Pepper, ground nutmeg, and several sprigs of chervil

Preparation:

1. Wash the asparagus, peel all of the white stalks and only the lower third of the green stalks, and cut off the woody ends. Cut the stalks into pieces 3/4 to 1 1/8 inches long. Boil water with salt, sugar, and one teaspoon butter and cook the asparagus in it 10 to 12 minutes, depending on thickness. Take them out, let them drip dry well, and keep the water cooking.

2. Heat the rest of the butter in a pot. Sift the flour in and immediately stir with a basting brush. Gradually add 3 cups of asparagus water, stirring constantly.

3. Bring the soup to a boil, stir in the vegetable broth powder, and let cook briefly.

4. Wash the chervil, shake dry, and chop fine. Stir the wine and sour cream into the soup. Flavor with the chervil, salt, pepper, and some ground nutmeg.

5. Add the asparagus pieces and serve the soup in bowls or cups.

TIP: A Special Tea Joy—A cup of stimulating, spicy Ayurvedisch herb tea tastes very good with this.

Ruegen Island *Asparagus* Soup

- 3/8 lb white asparagus
- 1/4 lb green asparagus
- 3 tablespoons butter
- 3 cups vegetable broth
- 2 tablespoons flour
- 1/2 cup white wine
- 1 cup sweet cream
- 1 teaspoon herbs in oil (such as thyme by Ostmann)
- 1/2 teaspoon salt
- 1 pinch ground white pepper and ground nutmeg
- 1/4 lb smoked trout fillets

Preparation:

1. Wash the asparagus, peel the white asparagus completely and only the lower third of the green, and cut off the woody ends. Cut the stalks into bite-size chunks.

2. Heat a tablespoon of butter, add the green asparagus pieces, steam, and take out. Put the white asparagus pieces in the remaining frying fat and steam them.

3. Pour in the broth, bring to a boil, and cook the asparagus pieces in it 10 to 12 minutes depending on thickness. Take out the asparagus, let drip dry, and keep the broth.

4. Heat the rest of the butter. Sift in the flour and immediately stir with a basting brush. Gradually pour in the asparagus broth, white wine, and cream. Boil and season with thyme in oil, salt, pepper, and nutmeg.

5. Cut the trout fillets into pieces and add them to the soup along with the asparagus pieces. Heat briefly and serve the soup in bowls or cups.

TIP: Serve with fresh bread.

Asparagus Tart

Preparation:

1. Prepare the dough according to directions on the package. Preheat oven to 350°F.

2. Wash the asparagus, peel the white asparagus completely and only the lower third of the green, and cut off the woody ends. Cut the stalks into bite-size chunks. Boil water with salt, sugar, and butter and cook the asparagus pieces in it 10 to 12 minutes, depending on thickness. Take asparagus out and let drip dry well.

3. Cut the cooked ham into strips.

4. Beat the eggs with milk and parsley, and season with salt and pepper.

5. Roll out the dough and place in a greased spring form with a diameter of 10 inches. Pour half of the filling into the spring form. Add the asparagus pieces and place the ham strips on the asparagus. Pour the rest of the filling over it, and scatter the pine nuts on it.

6. Sprinkle the cheese over the tart and bake in the oven 40 to 50 minutes. After half of the baking time, you may want to cover it with aluminum foil. Decorate with parsley and serve.

Recipe is for 12 servings

- 1/2 lb each white and green asparagus
- 1 pinch salt
- 1-2 teaspoons sugar
- 1 teaspoon butter
- Frozen pie crust
- 1/2 lb cooked ham
- Grease for the form
- 3/8 cup pine nuts
- 3/4 cup grated cheese
- Parsley

For the filling:

3 eggs · 1 cup milk · 3 tablespoons chopped parsley · salt and fresh ground pepper

Mini-Pizza with *Asparagus*

Preparation:

1. Preheat oven to 350°F. Sift the flour into a bowl, make a pit in the center, and crumble the yeast into it. Sprinkle with sugar, stir with 5 tablespoons of lukewarm water, cover, and leave in a warm place for about 20 minutes.

2. Add the rest of the ingredients and 3/8 cup lukewarm water to the dough, knead well, and let it set another 30 minutes.

3. Wash and peel the asparagus, cut off the woody ends, and cut into bite-size chunks. Boil water with salt, sugar, butter, and lemon juice and cook the asparagus pieces in it 10 to 12 minutes, depending on thickness. Take the asparagus out and let drip dry.

4. Stir the sour cream smooth and flavor with the Tzatziki herbs and chives. Wash the pearl onions, cut into rings, and add.

5. Wash the tomatoes and remove the stem area. Cut the tomatoes into slices and the cooked ham into strips. Roll out the dough for 12 mini-pizzas and coat with the stirred sour cream. Place the asparagus pieces, tomato slices, and ham strips on the pizzas, sprinkle with the cheese, and bake golden brown in the oven for about 20 minutes.

6. Sprinkle the basil in oil on the pizzas and serve decorated with chives.

For the dough:

· 5 cups flour
· 1 1/2 packets fresh yeast (.75 oz packets)
· 1/2 teaspoon sugar
· 1/2 cup lukewarm orange juice
· 1 egg
· 3 1/2 tablespoons soft butter

For the topping:

· 1/2 lb white asparagus
· 1 pinch salt
· 1-2 teaspoons sugar
· 1 teaspoon butter
· 1 tablespoon lemon juice
· 2 cups crème fraîche
· 2-3 teaspoons Tzatziki herbs
· 1 teaspoon chives, freezer-dried
· 4 pearl onions
· 8 slices of tomato (~1/4 inch thick)
· 1/4 lb cooked ham
· 3/4 cup grated cheese
· 4 teaspoons basil in oil (such as Ostmann)
· Fresh chives

Sole Dish with Green *Asparagus*

- 1 1/2 lbs fillet of sole (or flounder)
- 1 lb green asparagus
- 2-3 small potatoes (1 3/4" to 2 1/2")
- 1 shallot
- 7 tablespoons butter
- 1/3 cup white wine
- 1/2 cup chicken broth
- 1 small bay leaf
- 1 pinch pimento
- 1/4 bunch tarragon
- Salt and pepper

Preparation:

1. Wash the fish fillets under cold running water, dry with paper towel, and cut diagonally into strips 3/4 to 1 1/8 inches wide. Peel and cube the shallot.

2. Wash the asparagus, peel off the lower third, and cut off woody ends. Cut stalks into bite-size chunks. Wash the potatoes thoroughly so that the skin can be eaten and cut into thin slices.

3. Melt half of the butter in a coated pan and steam the vegetables in it for 2 minutes. Season with salt and pepper and pour the white wine over them. Add the chicken broth, laurel leaf, and pimento and steam covered 8 to 10 minutes.

4. Wash the tarragon, shake dry, and chop coarsely. Salt and pepper the fish strips; add to the vegetables along with the tarragon and heat together for 3 minutes.

5. Cut the rest of the butter into small cubes, carefully fold into the fish pan, and tip so that the juice is lightly bound. Season to taste and serve.

TIP: From Green Make White — Naturally you can always replace the green asparagus with white. Just remember that white asparagus must be completely peeled and cooked 10 to 15 minutes, depending on thickness. It will stay white with a teaspoon of lemon juice in the asparagus broth.

Asparagus with Pancakes and Herb Sauce

For the pancakes:

- 1 1/2 cups wheat flour
- 1 pinch salt
- 2 eggs
- 1 cup milk
- 1 teaspoon lemon juice
- 4 tablespoons butter
- 1/4 lb cooked ham
- 1/4 lb sliced salmon

For the Asparagus:

- 1 3/4 lbs white asparagus
- 1 pinch salt
- 1-2 teaspoons sugar
- 1 teaspoon butter
- 1 tablespoon lemon juice

For the Sauce:

- 2/3 cup butter
- 2 heaping tablespoons flour
- Salt and lemon juice
- 3 egg yolks
- 2 teaspoons chopped parsley
- 2 teaspoons chervil
- 2 teaspoons tarragon

Preparation:

1. Sift the flour into a bowl and mix well with the salt. Add the eggs and milk and beat to a smooth, lump-free batter. Let it settle well and then add the lemon juice.

2. Heat a tablespoon of butter in a pan, pour in a quarter of the batter, and make a pancake. Make three more pancakes in the rest of the butter and keep them warm.

3. Wash, peel, and trim the woody ends off the asparagus. Boil water with salt, sugar, butter, and lemon juice. Cook the asparagus in it for 10 to 15 minutes, depending on its thickness. Take asparagus out, let drip dry, and keep warm in the oven at 200°F.

4. Heat 7 tablespoons of butter in a pot for the sauce. Sift in the flour and immediately stir with a basting brush. Gradually add 1 1/2 cups of very hot water, stirring steadily. Season with salt and lemon juice, heat briefly, and take off the stove.

5. Stir in the rest of the butter, egg yolks, and herbs and season the sauce again.

6. Cover two pancakes with ham and two with salmon. Put the asparagus on the pancakes complete or in pieces and serve with herb sauce.

TIP: Bad Heilbrunner brand gourmet tea goes nicely with these.

Asparagus with Dumplings au Gratin

Preparation:

1. Preheat oven to 350°F.

2. Wash the asparagus, peel all of the white stalks and only the lower third of the green, and cut off woody ends. Cut stalks into pieces about 2 inches long. Boil water with salt, sugar, and butter and cook the asparagus in it for 10 to 12 minutes, depending on thickness. Take asparagus out and let them dry well. Keep the asparagus broth.

3. Prepare the mini-dumplings according to the package instructions and cut the ham into strips.

4. Heat the butter in a pot and sauté the flour lightly in it. Pour in the milk and 1 cup of the asparagus broth, boil, and season with salt, pepper, and ground nutmeg.

5. Wash the pearl onions and cut them into fine rings. Mix half of them into the sauce.

6. Put the asparagus pieces, dumplings, and ham strips into a gratin form, or similar 9 x 11 inch pan, and pour the sauce over them. Sprinkle cheese over it and bake about 30 to 35 minutes until golden brown. Scatter the rest of the pearl onions over the gratin and serve decorated with parsley.

For the Dumpling:

- 1 lb each white and green asparagus
- 1 pinch salt
- 1-2 teaspoons sugar
- 1 teaspoon butter
- One 14 oz package of mini-potato dumplings
- 1/4 lb Parma ham
- Parsley

For the Gratin Sauce:

- 2 tablespoons butter
- 3 tablespoons flour
- 1/2 cup milk (1.5% fat)
- 6 pearl onions
- 1/2 cup grated low-fat cheese
- Salt, freshly ground pepper, and ground nutmeg

For the Asparagus:

- 2 lbs white asparagus
- 2/3 cup vegetable broth
- 1/3 cup buckwheat flour
- 1/2 cup wheat flour
- 1/2 cup soft oatmeal
- 1 teaspoon turmeric
- 1 teaspoon ginger, freshly grated
- 1/2 teaspoon salt
- 1 medium egg yolk
- 3/4 cup coarse oatmeal
- 1 tablespoon vegetable oil

For the salad:

- One 8 oz package of mixed lettuce
- 4 tomatoes
- 4 tablespoons balsamic vinegar
- 3 tablespoons iodized salt and pepper
- 1 pinch sugar

Asparagus Rolls Gratiné

Preparation:

1. Preheat oven to 450°F.

2. Stir the sifted flour with the eggs for the crepes. Add 1 cup milk and stir. Melt the butter in a pot, let it cool somewhat, and mix it into the dough. Season the dough with Maggi Herb Mixture No. 1 and let stand for 10 minutes.

3. Heat the oil in a coated pan and bake six thin crepes from the dough in it, one at a time.

4. Wash the asparagus, peel the lower third, and cut off woody ends. Boil water with seasoning salt, sugar, and butter and cook the asparagus in it 8 to 10 minutes, depending on thickness. Take out and let drip-dry.

5. For the sauce, bring 1 cup water to a boil with Maggi fix and Frisch Spaghetti Napoli, and cook for a minute over low heat, stirring now and then. Put the sauce in a 8 x 11 inch baking form.

6. Mix the cottage cheese and half the Parmesan with a hand-mixer. Add the rest of the milk and flavor to taste with the Maggi herbs.

7. Coat the crepes thinly with the cottage cheese cream. Put 2 asparagus stalks on each crepe and roll them up tightly. Cut the rolled crepes into pieces 1 1/2 inches long and set them in the baking form upright, side by side.

8. Sprinkle on the rest of the Parmesan and let brown in the oven about 10 minutes.

For the Crepes:

- 1 1/2 cups flour
- 2 eggs
- 1 1/8 cups milk
- 2 tablespoons butter
- Maggi Herb Mixture No. 1
- Roasted meat
- 1 teaspoon sunflower oil
- 7/8 cup cottage cheese
- 1/4 cup grated Parmesan

For the Asparagus:

- 1 lb green asparagus
- 1 pinch seasoning salt
- 1-2 teaspoons sugar
- 1 teaspoon butter

For the sauce:

- 1 package of Maggi Fix and Fresh Spaghetti Napoli, or similar product

TIP: From Green to White—Naturally, you can always replace the green asparagus with white. Just remember that the white asparagus must be completely peeled and cooked 10 to 15 minutes depending on thickness. It will remain white with one tablespoon of lemon juice in the broth.

Arctic Char and Caramelized *Asparagus*

For the Asparagus:

- 2 1/4 lbs white asparagus
- 1 pinch salt
- 1-2 teaspoons sugar
- 1 tablespoon butter
- 3 tablespoons lemon juice
- 2 tablespoons brown sugar
- Parsley

For the Fish Fillets:

- 4 arctic char fillets of about 1/4 lb each
- 1/2 lb sliced Black Forest ham
- 1 tablespoon butter
- Salt, freshly ground pepper, and lemon juice

Preparation:

1. Wash and peel the asparagus and cut off woody ends. Boil water with salt, sugar, butter, and 2 tablespoons of lemon juice, and cook the asparagus in it for 10 to 15 minutes depending on the thickness. Take asparagus out, let it dry well, and keep it warm in the oven at 200°F.

2. Wash the char fillets under cold running water and pat dry with paper towels. Season with salt and pepper, sprinkle with lemon juice, and wrap them in ham. Fry about 5 minutes on each side in the heated butter.

3. Heat the brown sugar in a pan, put the asparagus in, and caramelize it. Sprinkle the rest of the lemon juice on the asparagus and season with salt.

4. Arrange the asparagus and char fillets on plates and serve decorated with parsley.

TIP: Fried potatoes go well with this dish.

Piecrust *Asparagus* Pockets

*Recipe is for 10 servings

- 1/2 lb each white and green asparagus
- 1 tablespoon butter
- 3/8 cup broth
- 1 package (~1 pound) frozen puff pastry
- 2 shallots
- Grated rind and juice from half an orange
- 7/8 cup cottage cheese
- 1/2 teaspoon mild mustard
- 1 cup cubed ham
- 1 egg, salt, and freshly ground pepper

Preparation:

1. Preheat oven to 400°F.

2. Wash the asparagus, peel the white completely and the lower third of the green, and cut off woody ends. Cut the stalks into pieces about 3/4 inch long and fry them in the heated butter. Pour in the broth and cook covered 5 to 10 minutes. Take asparagus out and let drip dry.

3. Prepare the pie crust as directed on the package.

4. Peel the shallots and cube finely. Mix the cottage cheese with the orange zest and juice, season to taste with salt and pepper, and mix with the ham cubes, asparagus, and shallots. Divide this filling among the crusts.

5. Separate the egg and paint the crust edges with the egg white. Fold the crusts together into bags and paint with the beaten egg yolk. Place on a sheet lined with baking paper and bake 20 to 30 minutes until golden brown.

Asparagus in a Crisp Coat of Oats

Preparation:

1. Butter to grease the form.

2. Preheat oven to 350°F. Mix eggs with the sifted flour, oatmeal, milk, mineral water, and salt to a smooth batter and let it rise for 30 minutes.

3. Heat a tablespoon of butter in a pan and scatter a tablespoon of oatmeal in it. Add 1/8 of the batter and bake a thin pancake. Make seven more pancakes in this manner and keep warm.

4. Wash, peel, and trim the woody ends off the asparagus. Boil water with salt, sugar, butter, and lemon juice. Cook the asparagus in it for 10 to 15 minutes, depending on its thickness. Take asparagus out and let drip-dry.

5. Wash the parsley and chives for the filling, shake dry, and cut fine. Cut the mozzarella into small cubes and mix with the sour cream and herbs. Save some chives for decoration. Season to taste with salt, pepper, sugar, and lemon juice.

6. For the sauce, mix the cream with the egg yolk, nutmeg, salt, and pepper. Grease a baking form and place 5 to 7 stalks of asparagus in the middle of each pancake, add 2 or 3 tablespoons of the filling, and roll them up.

7. Layer the pancake rolls in the form, pour the sauce over them, and scatter Parmesan cheese on top. Bake them a crisp brown in the oven about 12 minutes and decorate with the remaining chives. Serve ham alongside them.

For the Pancakes:

· 2 medium eggs
· 7/8 cup wheat flour
· 1/4 cup coarse oatmeal
· 1/4 tablespoon milk
· 1/4 tablespoon mineral water
· 1 pinch salt
· 8 tablespoons butter
· 8 tablespoons coarse oatmeal for baking

For the Asparagus:

· 2 1/4 lbs white asparagus
· 1 pinch of salt
· 1-2 teaspoons sugar
· 1 tablespoon butter
· 2 tablespoons lemon juice

For the Filling:

· 2 cups mozzarella (cubed)
· 2 tablespoons sour cream
· 1/2 bunch parsley
· 1/2 bunch chives
· Salt, pepper, and sugar
· 1 tablespoon lemon juice

For the Sauce:

· 3 tablespoons sour cream
· 1 medium egg yolk
· Ground nutmeg, salt, and pepper
· 3 tablespoons grated Parmesan cheese

Potato Noodle *Asparagus* Dish

Preparation:

1. Wash the asparagus, peel the white completely and the bottom third of the green, trim woody ends, and cut into bite-size chunks. Boil water with salt, sugar, and butter and cook the asparagus in it 10 to 12 minutes depending on thickness. Take asparagus out and let drip-dry. Keep the asparagus broth.

2. Wash the beef fillet under cold running water, pat dry with paper towels, and cut into strips. Peel the garlic, press it and mix it with the fillet, adding pepper and thyme.

3. Peel the shallots and cut into strips. Heat the oil, fry the beef strips and potato noodles in it, and then take them out. Steam the shallots in the remaining frying fat, add the asparagus, beef, and noodles, and heat briefly.

4. For the sauce, boil 1 cup asparagus broth with the vegetable broth and cream and let it cook down somewhat. You may want to thicken it with some light gravy thickener.

5. Wash the bear's garlic, shake dry, and cut into strips. Cut the vanilla pod lengthwise and take out the pulp. Refine the sauce with vanilla and bear's garlic and season with the herbs.

6. Garnish with parsley and serve with sauce.

*Recipe serves 2-3

- 2/3 lb each white and green asparagus
- 1 pinch of salt
- 1-2 teaspoons sugar
- 1 teaspoon butter
- 1/2 lb beef
- 1 garlic clove
- 2 shallots
- 1 teaspoon vegetable oil
- One 12 oz package of potato noodles
- Coarsely ground pepper, well-chopped thyme, and parsley

For the Sauce:

- 7/8 cup vegetable broth
- 1/4 cup low-fat sweet cream for cooking
- Light gravy thickener
- Several leaves of bear's garlic (or bear's garlic pesto)
- 1 vanilla bean pod
- Coarsely ground pepper
- Finely chopped thyme

Asparagus Variations

Asparagus can be combined with many other foods. Here are two of the many possible variations from which to choose: asparagus with kratzete, crepes that are cut into strips, and asparagus with potato pancakes.

Prepare the asparagus much in the same manner as in most of the previous dishes, with the following ingredients:

- 4 1/2 lbs white asparagus
- 1 pinch salt
- 1-2 teaspoons sugar
- 1 tablespoon butter
- 2 tablespoons lemon juice

Then, wash, peel, and cut off woody ends. Boil water with salt, sugar, butter, and lemon juice and cook the asparagus for 10 to 15 minutes depending on thickness. Take asparagus out, let it drip-dry, and keep warm in the oven at 200°F.

Variation 1: Asparagus with Kratzete

Preparation

1. Separate the eggs and beat the egg yolk to a froth. Add the milk, flour, and salad greens to the oil. Beat the egg white stiff and fold in.

2. Heat a tablespoon of butter in a pan, pour in a quarter of the batter, and make a pancake. After the first turning, "scratch" it into pieces with a flipper and keep warm. Make three more pancakes in the remaining butter and scratch them into pieces.

3. Stir the dip mix with the cottage cheese and yogurt. Arrange the asparagus with the kratzete and dip on plates and serve.

Variation 2: Asparagus with Potato Pancakes

Preparation:

1. Wash and peel the potatoes, peel the onions, and grate both. Mix with the eggs and season with salt, pepper, and nutmeg.

2. Heat some oil in a pan and fry crisp golden-brown potato pancakes, one after another, from the potato batter.

3. Stir the dip mix with the crème frâiche. Arrange the asparagus on plates with the potato pancakes, ham, and dip, and serve.

Variation 1: Asparagus with Kratzete

For the Kratzete:

- 4 eggs
- 1 1/3 cups milk
- 2 cups flour
- 1-2 teaspoons herbs in oil
- 4 tablespoons butter

For the Dip:

- 1 package herb garlic dip mix
- 1/2 cup cottage cheese
- 1/2 cup low-fat yogurt

Variation 2: Asparagus with Potato Pancakes

For the Potato Pancakes:

- 1 3/4 lbs potatoes
- 1 onion
- 2 eggs
- 1 teaspoon salt
- 1/4 teaspoon ground white pepper
- 1 pinch ground nutmeg
- 4 tablespoons cooking oil

TIP: Adding 8 slices of smoked or baked ham makes a good side dish.

For the Dip:

- 1 package spring herb dip mix
- 1 cup crème fraîche

Asparagus Ham Salad "Primavera"

Preparation:

1. Wash the asparagus, peel the white completely and the lower third of the green, and cut off woody ends. Cut stalks into bite-size chunks. Boil water with salt, sugar, and butter and cook the asparagus in it 10 to 12 minutes, depending on thickness. Take out and let drip-dry.

2. Wash the cherry tomatoes and helve or quarter depending on size. Wash the pearl onions and cut into fine rings. Wash the leaf lettuce and cut into bite-size chunks.

3. Mix the vinegar with mustard, honey, vegetable broth, and chive pieces and season with salt and pepper. Then stir in the olive oil.

4. Arrange the salad greens on four large plates. Apportion the asparagus, tomatoes, and onion rings on them. Sprinkle with dressing and add rolled ham slices.

TIP: Fried baguette is a good accompaniment.

For the Salad:

- 1 lb each white and green asparagus
- 1 pinch salt
- 1-2 teaspoons sugar
- 1 tablespoon butter
- 1 1/2 cups cherry tomatoes
- 1/2 bunch pearl onions
- One 10 oz package mixed salad greens
- 1/2 lb sliced ham

For the Dressing:

- 2-3 tablespoons white balsamic vinegar
- 2 teaspoons mustard
- 2 teaspoons honey
- 3/8 cup vegetable broth
- 2 tablespoons cut chives
- 2 tablespoons olive oil
- Salt and pepper

For the Asparagus:

- 2 1/4 lbs white asparagus
- 1 pinch salt
- 1-2 teaspoons sugar
- 1 tablespoon butter
- 2 tablespoons lemon juice

For the Ragout:

- 8 shrimp without heads
- 1 onion and 1 star anise
- 1 teaspoon garlic powder
- 2 tablespoons butter
- 1 pinch ground saffron
- 7/8 cups crème fraîche
- 1/2 teaspoon lemon pepper
- 1/4 teaspoon ground cayenne pepper
- Salt and sugar
- 1-2 tablespoons light gravy thickener
- 2 level teaspoons ground chervil

For the Risotto:

- 4 small shallots
- 2 tablespoons olive oil
- 1/2 teaspoon garlic powder
- 2 pinches powdered vanilla
- 1/2 cup risotto rice
- 1/4 cup white wine
- 1 cup chicken broth
- 2 3/4 tablespoons sherry
- 1/4 cup marscapone
- 1/4 cup butter
- 1/4 cup ground Parmesan

Asparagus Scampi Ragout with Risotto

Preparation:

1. Wash, peel, and trim woody ends off the asparagus and cut the stalks into bite-size chunks. Boil water with salt, sugar, butter, and lemon juice and cook the asparagus 10 to 12 minutes depending on thickness. Take asparagus out and let drip-dry. Keep the asparagus broth.

2. Wash the shrimp under cold running water and pat dry with paper towels. Take the meat out of the shells, cut in half lengthwise, and remove the innards.

3. Peel the onion and cube coarsely. Cook the onion cubes with the shrimp shells, star anise, garlic, asparagus broth, butter, and saffron. Simmer uncovered over low heat about 15 minutes.

4. Strain the asparagus broth through a sieve and stir smooth with the fresh cream. Season with the lemon pepper, salt, cayenne pepper, and sugar, and thicken with gravy thickener. Add the asparagus and shrimp and heat about 2 minutes. Then add the chervil.

5. Peel the shallots for the risotto and cut into fine cubes. Heat the oil and steam the shallot cubes with the garlic and the vanilla aroma. Add the rice and steam until glassy.

6. Pour in the wine, broth, and sherry and let the rice absorb, stirring at times, about 15 minutes. Refine the risotto with marscapone, butter, and Parmesan.

7. Apportion the ragout with the risotto and serve garnished with spring herbs and star anise.

For the Asparagus:

- 1 lb each white and green asparagus
- 1 pinch salt
- 1-2 teaspoons sugar
- 1 tablespoon butter
- 1 1/3 lbs new potatoes
- 1/2 lb ham strips
- Grease for the form
- 1 cup grated herb cheese
- Parsley

For the Gratin Sauce:

- 1 cup sweet cream
- 4 eggs
- Salt and freshly ground pepper
- Ground nutmeg

Asparagus au Gratin

Preparation:

1. Preheat oven to 350°F.

2. Wash the asparagus, peel the white completely and the lower third of the green, cut off woody ends. Cut the asparagus into bite-size chunks. Boil water with salt, sugar, and butter, and cook the asparagus 10 to 12 minutes depending on thickness. Take out and let drip-dry.

3. Wash, peel, and slice the potatoes. Layer the sliced potatoes, asparagus pieces, and ham strips in a greased form.

4. Stir the cream with the eggs, season with salt, pepper, and nutmeg, and pour over the gratin.

5. Scatter cheese on the gratin, bake golden brown about 40 to 50 minutes, and serve decorated with parsley.

Asparagus with Almond Piccata

For the Asparagus:

- 3 1/3 lbs white asparagus
- 1 pinch salt
- 1-2 teaspoons sugar
- 1 tablespoon butter
- 2 tablespoons lemon juice

For the Sauce:

- 2 bunches parsley
- 8 anchovy fillets
- 2 tablespoons lemon juice
- 3 tablespoons grated California almonds
- 1/2 cup olive oil
- Salt and pepper

For the Piccata:

- 2 eggs
- 1/3 cup grated Parmesan
- 1/2 cup California almond slices
- 8 thin veal cutlets (~1/8 lb each)
- Salt, pepper, flour, and clarified butter

TIP: Piccata for Vegetarians—You can also make the cheese-almond mixture as small dumplings without the filling. Melt some butter in a hot-coated pan and put the dumplings in with a tablespoon. Fry 2 minutes, turn, and fry golden brown for two more minutes.

Preparation:

1. Wash, peel, and cut the woody ends off the asparagus. Boil water with salt, sugar, butter, and lemon juice, and cook the asparagus in it 10 to 15 minutes, depending on thickness. Take asparagus out, let drip-dry, and keep warm in the oven at 200°F.

2. For the sauce, wash the parsley, shake dry, and pick off the stems. Wash the anchovy fillets under cold running water and pat dry with paper towels. Puree along with the parsley, lemon juice, and grated almonds, adding salt so the sauce remains nicely green. Gradually add olive oil and finally season with salt and pepper.

3. Beat the eggs with the Parmesan and fold in the sliced almonds. Wash the veal cutlets under cold running water and pat dry with paper towels. Salt and pepper lightly, coat with flour, and drag through the cheese-almond mixture.

4. Heat the clarified butter in a coated pan and fry the Piccata in it for 5 to 6 minutes, turning after 2 to 3 minutes.

5. Arrange the asparagus with the Piccata and sauce on plates and serve decorated with parsley.

TIP: Salted potatoes or gnocchi goes well with this dish.

Fried Salmon on *Asparagus*

For the Salmon:

- 1 1/3 lbs salmon fillet
- 3 garlic cloves
- 1 bunch parsley
- 1 untreated lime
- 3/8 cup grated Parmesan
- 3 tablespoons olive oil
- 1/4 cup pine nuts
- Salt and pepper

For the Asparagus:

- 1 2/3 lbs each white and green asparagus
- 1 pinch salt
- 1-2 teaspoons sugar
- 1 tablespoon butter

Preparation:

1. Wash the salmon under cold running water, pat dry with paper towels, and cut into four portions.

2. Peel the garlic and cut into slices. Wash the parsley, shake dry, and cut fine. Wash the lime hot, rub very dry, and cut into slices. Grate the Parmesan finely.

3. Wash the asparagus, peel the white completely and the lower third of the green, cut off woody ends. Boil water with salt, sugar, and butter, and cook the green asparagus in it 8 to 12 minutes and the white 10 to 15 minutes, depending on thickness. Take asparagus out, let drip-dry, and keep warm in the oven at 200°F.

4. Heat the olive oil and fry the salmon in it on both sides about 5 minutes. After 4 minutes, add the lime and garlic slices and the pine nuts, and fry briefly. Season with parsley, salt, and pepper.

5. Arrange the asparagus on plates with the salmon and serve strewn with Parmesan.

TIP: You can serve pasta, such as penne, with this dish.

Chicken Breast with Cheese Crust on Green *Asparagus*

Preparation:

1. Preheat oven to 200°F. Cut the cheese into cubes and mix with the white bread crumbs and almonds.

2. Wash the chicken breasts under cold running water and pat dry with paper towels. Heat the oil in a pan and fry the chicken breasts about 2 minutes on each side at medium heat. Let them cook juicily in the oven about 20 minutes, take out, and switch the oven to the broiler function.

3. Season the chicken breasts with salt and pepper. Coat the upper sides with pesto. Press 1/4 of the cheese flat with your hands and lay it on the pesto.

4. Put the chicken breasts with the cheese-pesto on top in an oven-proof bowl. Bake on the lowest oven rack under the broiler about 5 minutes.

5. Wash the asparagus, peel the bottom third, and cut off woody ends. Quarter the stalks diagonally. Boil water with salt, sugar, and butter, and cook the asparagus pieces in it 10 to 12 minutes, depending on thickness. Take out and let drip-dry.

6. Wash and halve the cherry tomatoes. Peel and halve the garlic. Warm the asparagus, tomatoes, garlic, and lemon rind in the broth. Remove the garlic and lemon rind and season the vegetables with salt and pepper. Scatter the parsley on it and add the butter.

7. Arrange the asparagus vegetables on plates and place a cut-up chicken breast on each. Serve garnished with spring herbs.

TIP: Make White from Green—Naturally you can always replace the green asparagus with white. Just be sure to peel the white asparagus completely and cook 10 to 15 minutes, depending on thickness. With 1 tablespoon of lemon juice in the broth, it will stay white.

For the Chicken Breast:

- 1 1/3 cup soft cheese cubed
- 7/8 cup white bread crumbs
- 1/3 cup blanched ground almonds
- 4 chicken breasts skinned (1/4 lb to 1/3 lb each)
- 1 tablespoon oil
- 3-4 tablespoons bear's garlic pesto
- Salt and freshly ground black pepper

For the Asparagus:

- 7/8 lbs green asparagus
- 1 pinch of salt
- 1-2 teaspoons sugar
- 1 teaspoon butter

For the Vegetables:

- 1 cup cherry tomatoes
- 1 garlic clove
- 1 strip of untreated lemon rind
- 5-6 tablespoons vegetable broth
- 1 tablespoon chopped parsley
- 1 tablespoon butter
- Salt and freshly ground black pepper

Asparagus Quiche Lorraine with Tarragon

For the Dough:

- 2 cups whole-grain flour
- 1/2 cup cold butter
- 2 eggs
- 1/2 cup cottage cheese
- 1 pinch salt

For the Asparagus:

- 1 lb white asparagus
- 1 pinch salt
- 1-2 teaspoons sugar
- 1 teaspoon butter
- 1 tablespoon lemon juice

For the Sauce:

- 1/2 cup sweet cream
- 2 tablespoons sour cream
- 2 eggs
- 1 bunch tarragon
- 1/2 bunch parsley
- Salt and freshly ground white pepper
- Freshly ground nutmeg

Preparation:

1. Be sure to use flour for the work surface and butter to grease the sheet.

2. Preheat oven to 350°F. Knead the sifted flour and butter (cut small) to a smooth dough with eggs, cottage cheese, and salt. Wrap the dough in clear, plastic wrap and leave in a cool place for an hour.

3. Wash and peel the asparagus and cut off woody ends. Boil water with salt, sugar, butter, and lemon juice, and cook the asparagus in it about 10 minutes. Take out and let drip-dry.

4. Roll out the dough about 3/8 inch thick on a floured surface and place it in a greased baking sheet. Divide the asparagus stalks evenly on it.

5. Wash the tarragon and celery, shake dry, and chop. Mix the cream, thin sour cream, and eggs with the herbs. Season with salt, pepper, and nutmeg and pour over the asparagus. Bake golden brown in the oven about 50 minutes, covering the edges with aluminum foil after about 30 minutes. Serve the asparagus cake lukewarm.

Strawberries

History and Origin

Wild strawberries were already known to our ancient ancestors in the latest Stone Age. In the Middle Ages, there were large fields on which strawberries were cultivated. The large-fruited garden berry that we know today, though, has existed for only about 200 years. In America, it developed from a crossing of the small scarlet strawberry and the large-fruited Chilean strawberry.

The small wild strawberry is found in Europe and northern Asia along wood edges as well as in light coniferous and deciduous forests and—usually very expensively—at weekly markets.

Varieties and Types

There are more than a thousand varieties with differing soil and climate requirements and different appearance, flavor, and growth. Unfortunately, there are many among them that suit the requirements of the growers and sellers better than those of the consumer: big, attractive fruits that can withstand long transport routes and several days of storage problem-free. These fruits are often scarcely juicy and their consistency resembles that of bubble-gum... to say nothing of their lack of aroma and fragrance!

The traditional types are not being grown as often commercially. Thus you will rarely find the once frequently grown, aromatic "Senga Sengana" type, for it is sensitive and not attractive enough for the trade. Aromatic types like "Mieze Schindler" were completely banned from the commercial fields and are regarded today as purely amateur types for the hobby gardener.

Meanwhile, though, efforts to get back to the roots have become known: from Spain in recent years, for example, have come appealing fruits that are not only robust, but also taste like strawberries. Perhaps the development of a strawberry that not only looks good, but also is insensitive to transport and has the aroma of earlier types will be created.

Figure-friendly strawberries are rich in vitamins and minerals. They have a Vitamin C content of 60 mg per 100 grams of fruit and contain valuable minerals such as calcium, potassium, phosphorus, and iron. Not without reason are strawberries seen in folk medicine as an effective antidote to anemia. Because of their high silicic acid content, they are recommended for the relief of gout and rheumatism. Not only are they healthy little fruits, but fresh strawberries with a bit of sugar or whipped cream rank among the most delicious joys of early summer.

Growing, Harvesting, and Buying

The time to harvest strawberries is relatively short. They are generally harvested from May to July, but there are also types that can be harvested until October. For greenhouse strawberries, the season begins in March.

The first strawberries from Spanish growers arrive in our stores in January, joined by those from Italy in March. In flavor, though, they cannot compare with our homegrown fruits.

Whoever cannot grow strawberries in their own garden should not feel disadvantaged. He can pick his strawberries at one of the many pick-your-own farms or buy them directly from the grower. In any case, they are worth the effort. As a rule, the farms still grow aromatic types like "Senga Sengana." Then you can also tell that a sun-ripened, freshly picked strawberry tastes incomparably much better. The more punctually strawberries are picked, the better they taste. For the fruits do not ripen afterward!

Strawberries come from Israel from November to February. If at least 2/3 of the fruit surface is red, the berries can be enjoyed, but they only develop their full aroma when they are completely red.

Another possibility of avoiding disappointments when buying strawberries is to go to weekly markets. Here local farmers often offer their wares in small quantities, and the chance of being able to buy aromatic strawberries is quite great. Usually it does not take longer than one day until the picked strawberries get from the field to the market. The strawberry is very sensitive and does not like to age. With their full aroma and unmistakable flavor, if strawberries are enjoyed when fresh, the trouble of quick transport from the field to the fruit dish is worthwhile.

Strawberries in the Kitchen

Preservation:

Strawberries are extremely sensitive and should be transported carefully and either eaten or prepared immediately. They are sensitive to pressure and get moldy quickly, so pick out damaged berries. Otherwise, the berries should be stored, if possible, unwashed and covered in a cool place or in the produce drawer of the refrigerator (and taken out half an hour before eating).

Preparation:

You should never wash strawberries with a strong stream of water, just dip them briefly in cold water. The washed berries should be allowed to drip-dry or be carefully patted dry. Only after washing should stems and leaves be removed; otherwise the berries will "bleed," meaning that the juice runs out and the berries lose their flavor and become watery. Put sugar on the berries just shortly before eating, or they will lose too much juice and become soft and limp.

Storage:

Strawberries can be frozen very well! So that the pressure-sensitive berries do not turn into an amorphous mass, you should pre-freeze them after cleaning. Grilling pans are well suited for this; arrange the berries as if on a plate and slide them into the freezer. The berries must not move. You can also sugar the berries (1/2 to 1 cup granulated or powdered sugar per 2 1/4 lbs of berries) before putting them in a freezer bag.

Of course the most delicious berries and the most thorough treatment mean nothing if the frozen berries are not packed carefully. Freezer bags with wide openings and practical bottoms, are reliable and easy to fill. The three-layer foil protects the fruit from freezer burn. The bags can be closed very simply with special clamps or closing clips. As a result, the strawberries can be stored for a year.

DID YOU KNOW?... The strawberry is second only to the apple as the Germans' favorite fruit. The average consumption is about 2 pounds per year.

An absolutely classic way to bring the "queen of fruits" to the table in winter is in the form of homemade strawberry jam. It makes the breakfast roll taste twice as good and it always enjoys the greatest popularity.

Strawberry Jam

Ingredients

· 1 1/8 lbs (~1 1/2 pints) fresh aromatic strawberries
· 1 1/8 lbs jelly sugar
· 2 vanilla bean pods

Preparation:

1. Blend the washed and cleaned strawberries in the mixer.

2. Mix the berries with the jelly sugar in a bowl and cook for about 5 minutes, stirring often, so the mixture does not scorch.

3. Cut the vanilla pods lengthwise, take out the pulp, and stir it into the strawberries.

4. Rinse the jelly glasses in hot water and fill them with the strawberry mixture.

5. Seal the glasses immediately and let them set a few minutes, so that no germs survive.

The *Strawberry* Diet

Extent of the diet: 3 days
Meals per day: 5
Average calorie intake per day: 1,200

Strawberries are ideal for losing weight. They contain 32 calories per 100 grams, are filling, and taste great. Strawberries are real vitamin bombs; they're rich in Vitamin E, which contributes to cell protection, Vitamin C, and the B vitamins. They also contain important minerals such as potassium, calcium, magnesium, and iron. The potassium helps in weight loss — it activates the work of the kidneys, promoting the body's water loss.
With only 1,200 calories per day, you will soon lose weight on a strawberry diet — and without going hungry. Besides the main meals, you have two small snacks. In addition to the drinks listed in the diet plan, you should drink plenty of fluid, at least 2 liters per day. It is best to choose calorie-free drinks such as tea or mineral water. Sweetened drinks are hidden calorie bombs and should be avoided during weight-loss programs. Dinkula, the fermented sour-milk enzyme drink, is also good. It promotes digestion and strengthens the immune system. Dinkula can be found in most health-food stores.

Diet Evaluation

Weight Loss	*****
Satiation	****
Nutrition	****
Digestion	****
Practicality	*****
Convenience	****
Cost	*****

DAY ONE

Total: 1,183 calories, 54.3 grams protein, 24.9 grams fat, 174.8 grams carbohydrate

Breakfast:

Strawberry-Kiwi Cereal

312 calories, 10.5 grams protein, 2.1 grams fat, 58.1 grams carbohydrate

- 1/4 lb strawberries
- 1 kiwi
- 1/2 grapefruit
- 1 2/3 cups corn flakes
- 2/3 cup buttermilk

Wash, clean, and halve the strawberries. Peel and cube the kiwi. Peel the grapefruit and cut into small pieces. Put the corn flakes in a deep bowl, mix in the fruits, pour on the buttermilk, and let stand briefly.

Snack:

Vitamin Cocktail

91 calories, 2.1 grams protein, 0.5 gram fat, 17.5 grams carbohydrate

- 1/2 grapefruit (from breakfast)
- 1 large orange
- 1/2 cup Dinkula
- 1 tablespoon bran

Juice the orange and grapefruit. Mix the juices with Dinkula and stir in the bran. Then drink.

Lunch:

Strawberry Pancakes

396 calories, 16.8 grams protein, 13.7 grams fat, 50.8 grams carbohydrate

- 1/3 cup wheat flour
- 2/3 cup skim milk
- 1 egg
- Sea salt and sweetener
- 2 teaspoons thistle oil
- 2 teaspoons instant vanilla sauce
- 1/4 lb strawberries
- 3/4 cup Dinkula

Mix half the milk with the egg, a pinch of salt, a few drops sweetener, and the sifted flour. Stir until smooth. Heat the oil in a coated pan and bake two pancakes, one after the other. Wash and clean the strawberries, cut into thin slices, and put on the pancakes. Mix the rest of the milk with the vanilla sauce powder, serve on the pancakes, and drink Dinkula.

Snack:

Fruited Bread

152 calories, 13.1 grams protein, 3.7 grams fat, 16.1 grams carbohydrate

- 2 slices whole-grain crispbread
- 1/3 cup cottage cheese
- 1/2 kiwi
- 1/8 cup strawberries

Spread the cottage cheese on the crispbread and add the kiwi and strawberry slices.

Dinner:

Fruit Salad

232 calories, 11.8 grams protein, 4.9 grams fat, 32.3 grams carbohydrate

- 1 orange and 1 kiwi
- 1/4 lb strawberries
- 1/2 cup low-fat yogurt
- 2 tablespoons orange nectar
- 1 tablespoon wheat flakes

Peel and fillet the orange, cut the kiwi into thin slices, and wash, clean, and quarter the strawberries. Mix the yogurt with orange nectar and wheat flakes and put on the fruit.

DAY TWO

Total: 1,201 calories, 57.5 grams protein, 22.4 grams fat, 185.4 grams carbohydrate

Breakfast:

Fit-Maker Breakfast

339 calories, 18.4 grams protein, 5.6 grams fat, 48.3 grams carbohydrate

- 1 slice whole wheat bread
- 1/2 cup cottage cheese
- 1 small orange
- 1/4 lb strawberries
- 3/4 cup buttermilk

Cut the slice of bread in half; spread with cottage cheese. Add the sliced strawberries or orange pieces and drink buttermilk.

Snack:

Strawberry Flip

104 calories, 7.9 grams protein, 1.3 grams fat, 13.9 grams carbohydrate

- 3/4 cup buttermilk
- 1/4 lb strawberries
- Lemon juice and sweetener

Puree the strawberries, mix with buttermilk, and flavor with some lemon juice and sweetener.

Lunch:

Fat Dumplings with Strawberries

368 calories, 19.6 grams protein, 12 grams fat, 44.4 grams carbohydrate

- 2/3 cup skim milk
- 1/8 cup oil
- 1/2 teaspoon vanilla sugar
- 1 pinch salt
- Sweetener
- 1 egg yolk
- 1/4 lb strawberries
- 1 tablespoon low-fat yogurt
- 3/4 cup Dinkula

Heat the milk and add the grease, vanilla sugar, and salt. Cook briefly, stirring constantly. Let cool briefly, then stir in the egg yolk and flavor with sweetener. Meanwhile, wash and clean the strawberries, slice, and add sweetener. Put several berry slices aside. From the cooled broth, make 3 dumplings (best done with two spoons) and put on a plate with the strawberry slices. Pour the strawberry yogurt over it. Drink Dinkula with it.

Snack:

Strawberry Shake

102 calories, 6.5 grams protein, 1.5 grams fat, 14.3 grams carbohydrate

- 1/3 lb strawberries
- 2/3 cup buttermilk
- Lemon juice and sweetener

Wash and clean strawberries, blend well with buttermilk in a mixer, and flavor with lemon juice and sweetener.

Dinner:

Fruit Salad

232 calories, 11.8 grams protein, 4.9 grams fat, 32.3 grams carbohydrate

- 1 orange
- 1 kiwi
- 1/4 lb strawberries
- 1/2 cup low-fat yogurt
- 2 tablespoons orange nectar
- 1 tablespoons wheat flakes

Peel and fillet the orange, cut kiwi into small pieces, and wash, clean, and quarter strawberries. Mix yogurt with orange nectar and wheat flakes and spread over the fruit.

DAY THREE

Total: 1,182 calories, 70.9 grams protein, 31.2 grams fat, 154.5 grams carbohydrate

Breakfast:

Strawberry-Banana Cereal

295 calories, 8.9 grams protein, 4.9 grams fat, 52.2 grams carbohydrate

- 3 tablespoons whole-grain oatmeal
- 1 tablespoon wheat bran
- 1/2 cup skim milk
- 1/4 cup strawberries
- 1 small slice pineapple and 1/2 of a banana

Mix the oatmeal and bran together and pour milk over it. Wash, clean, and halve the strawberries. Cut the half banana in slices and the pineapple slice in small pieces. (Save the second banana half for the snack.) Mix the fruit into the cereal.

Snack:

Kefir Drink

154 calories, 7.3 grams protein, 2.9 grams fat, 24.5 grams carbohydrate

- 1/2 cup low-fat Kefir
- 3/8 cup Dinkula
- 1/2 banana
- 1 tablespoon soft oatmeal
- Cinnamon

Blend the Kefir, Dinkula, banana, and oatmeal together well in a mixer, flavor with cinnamon (optional), and serve chilled.

Lunch:

Wellness Bread with Strawberries

256 calories, 15.9 grams protein, 3.4 grams fat, 38.3 grams carbohydrate

- 2 slices whole wheat bread
- 1/3 cup cottage cheese
- 1/4 lb strawberries
- 2 cups tea

Spread the cottage cheese on the bread. Wash, clean, and slice the strawberries and place them on the bread. Drink tea with it.

Snack:

Strawberry Cup with Pistachio

172 calories, 6.1 grams protein, 6.9 grams fat, 18.9 grams carbohydrate

- 3/8 cup strawberries
- 1/2 cup low-fat yogurt
- 1 teaspoon vanilla sugar
- 1 teaspoon pistachio
- 3/4 cup Dinkula

Wash, clean, and cut strawberries into bite-size chunks. Sweeten yogurt with vanilla sugar. Cut pistachios into small pieces. Place strawberries in a fruit cup, pour the yogurt over them, scatter the pistachios on top, and serve. Drink Dinkula with it.

Dinner:

Exotic Turkey Salad

305 calories, 32.7 grams protein, 13.1 grams fat, 20.6 grams carbohydrate

- 1/4 lb turkey breast
- 1 teaspoon thistle oil and cider vinegar
- Several drops of soy sauce
- 1/8 lb strawberries
- 2/3 fresh pineapple chunks
- 3 stalks celery
- 1/3 cup low-fat yogurt
- Pepper, curry powder, and sea salt

Wash turkey breast cold, pat dry and cut up, and brown in a pan greased with some oil. Take out and let drip on a marinade made of vinegar and soy sauce. Cut the fruits into small pieces and the celery into small slices. Fold the fruits and vegetables into the marinated meat. Season the curry with pepper, sea salt, and curry powder, and pour over the salad.

For the Gnocchi:

- 1 lb white russet potatoes
- 1 teaspoon salt
- 1/2 cup flour
- 1/3 cup wheat-germ semolina
- 1 egg yolk and 1 vanilla bean pod
- 2 tablespoons sugar
- 1/2 lb strawberries
- Fresh mint leaves

For the Fruit:

- 2/3 cup grated coconut
- 1 tablespoon butter
- 2 tablespoons honey
- 2 2/3 cups pineapple pieces
- 2 tablespoons chopped mint

Coconut Gnocchi with *Strawberries*

Preparation:

1. Wash the potatoes and cook in a covered pot with salt for about 20 minutes. Test with a sharp kitchen knife to see if they are done. Peel the potatoes, let cool, and then mash.

2. Mix the sifted flour, semolina, egg yolk, and sugar together. Cut the vanilla pod open lengthwise, take out the pulp, and add to the potatoes.

3. Make the dough into small balls, press with a fork, and blanch in boiling water until the gnocchi comes to the surface. Drain and cool with cold water.

4. Brown the shredded coconut briefly in a coated pan without fat. Caution—they burn quickly! Melt the butter in a pan, add the honey, and let it caramelize. Add the pineapple pieces with the juice, heat, and let the fluid reduce somewhat. Mix the gnocchi and the grated coconut and warm briefly.

5. Wash, clean, and slice the strawberries. Apportion the gnocchi and fruit sauce on plates and scatter the chopped mint on it. Serve garnished with strawberry slices and mint leaves.

*Unless otherwise noted, recipes are for four servings.

Strawberry Dream

Ingredients

· 1 1/8 lb strawberries
· 4 tablespoons sugar
· 1/2 package whipped cream stabilizer
· 1/2 cup sweet cream
· 1 cup low-fat yogurt
· 6 tablespoons Nutella
· Fresh lemon mint

*Recipe is for five servings

Preparation:

1. Wash, clean, and dice the strawberries. Save 5 small berries for decoration.

2. Puree half the diced strawberry with the sugar. Beat the whipped cream stabilizer stiff with 7 tablespoons of cream. Mix the yogurt with the strawberry puree and the rest of the diced strawberry and fold into the cream. Divide the mixture into 5 small portions and freeze for 2 hours.

3. Warm the Nutella with the rest of the cream, and spoon out 2/3 of it as mirrors on the plates. Let the forms defrost a little and put the contents onto the plates.

4. Halve the remaining strawberries and decorate each plate with two halves and some lemon zest. With a teaspoon, decorate the cakes with the remaining warmed Nutella.

Strawberry Biscuit Roll

Preparation:

1. Preheat oven to 350°F.

2. Separate the eggs for the dough and beat the yolks to a foam along with the sugar. Beat the egg whites stiff and fold into the egg-yolk/sugar mixture. Sift the flour and baking powder, mix, and carefully fold into the mixture.

3. Lay out the dough on a sheet lined with baking paper and roll it flat. Bake in the oven about 10 to 12 minutes.

4. Slide the hot biscuit bottom with the baking paper onto a clean dish-towel sprinkled with fine sugar. Put some cold water on the baking paper and carefully separate it. Roll up the still-warm biscuit bottom with the help of the towel and let it cool for about one hour.

5. For the filling, wash and clean the strawberries and puree them coarsely with the lemon juice and 1 ounce of sugar. Retain six strawberries for the decoration.

6. Soften and dissolve the gelatin in cold water, as directed on the package.

7. Beat the cream stiff with the rest of the sugar and let the whipped cream stabilizer trickle into it. Take out about 1 tablespoon of the cream and put into a sprayer with a star point for the decoration. Fold the strawberry puree and the gelatin into the remaining cream.

8. Roll out the biscuit material, coat with the strawberry-cream filling, and carefully roll it up. Quarter the remaining strawberries. Decorate the roll with dots of cream and the strawberry quarters. Refrigerate for at least 2 hours and decorate with lemon mint.

For the Dough:

- 3 eggs
- 2/3 cup sugar
- 1 1/8 cup instant flour
- 1 pinch baking powder

For the Filling:

- 2/3 lb strawberries
- 1 tablespoon lemon juice
- 1/4 cup sugar
- 6 sheets of gelatin
- 1 2/3 cups sweet cream
- 2 packages whipped cream stabilizer

Other ingredients

- Fine sugar and fresh, lemon mint

*Recipe is for 12 servings

Strawberry Semolina Muffins

Ingredients

- 1/2 lb strawberries
- 4 stalks of rhubarb
- 1/2 cup raw marzipan
- 2/3 cup butter
- 3/4 cup sugar
- 1 pinch salt
- 1/2 cup low-fat yogurt
- 1/2 cup soft wheat semolina
- 1 1/8 wheat flour
- 1 even teaspoon baking powder
- 3 eggs and grease for the form
- 2 teaspoons vanilla sugar
- 1 teaspoon sugar
- 3 tablespoons orange juice or liqueur
- Confectioners sugar

*Recipe is for 12 servings

Preparation:

1. Preheat oven to 350°F.

2. Wash, clean, and cut into small pieces the strawberries and rhubarb. Save a few pieces for the decoration.

3. Press the raw mass of marzipan and stir it smooth with the butter. Add sugar, salt, yogurt, semolina, and eggs, and stir. Sift the flour and baking powder, mix, and fold into the semolina.

4. Fold the rhubarb pieces and about 1/3 of the strawberry pieces into the dough. Put the dough in a greased muffin pan and bake about 35 minutes.

5. For the sauce, puree the rest of the strawberry pieces with both the sugar and vanilla sugar, and flavor with the orange juice or liqueur.

6. Put the muffins on plates with the sauce. Dust with confectioners sugar and decorate with the remaining pieces of fruit.

GOLD
PUDER

Ice Cream Sandwich Tower with *Strawberries*

Ingredients:

- 3 ice cream sandwiches
- 1/2 cup finely chopped California almonds
- 1 cup strawberries (quartered)
- 1/4 cup chocolate syrup

*Recipe is for 3 servings

Preparation:

1. Roll the ice cream sandwiches in the chopped almonds in a flat pan until their sides are completely covered with them. Stack the ice cream sandwiches on a small plate.

2. Wash, clean, and quarter the strawberries and divide them among the plate and sandwich tower.

3. Pour the chocolate sauce decoratively over the tower and serve the sandwich tower at once.

4. Leftover almonds can be scattered over the finished sandwich tower.

Cream Puffs with *Strawberry* Cream Filling

Preparation:

1. Preheat oven to 400°F.

2. Melt the butter with 1 cup water, the salt, and vanilla sugar. Add the sifted flour and stir until the dough comes loose from the bottom as a ball. Take the pot from the stove and stir in the eggs one at a time.

3. Using 2 spoons, make 12 heaps of dough on a sheet lined with baking paper and bake to a golden brown about 25 to 30 minutes. Immediately after baking, cut off the upper third of each cream puff and let it cool on a rack.

4. Soften and dissolve the gelatin in cold water according to the directions on the package. Wash, clean, and cube the strawberries and puree half of them. Mix the strawberry puree and cubes with the liqueur. Fold in the gelatin.

5. Beat the cream stiff with the sugar and vanilla sugar, and carefully fold into the strawberries as soon as they begin to gel.

6. Let the frosting mix melt in hot water according to the instructions on the package. Using a teaspoon, decorate the tops of the cream puffs with the frosting.

7. Distribute the strawberry cream on the lower parts of the cream puffs, put the tops on, and sprinkle with confectioners sugar for decoration.

For the Dough:

- 1/4 cup butter
- 1 pinch salt
- 1 package vanilla sugar
- 1 cup wheat flour
- 4 eggs

For the Filling:

- 3 sheets white gelatin
- 1/2 lb strawberries
- 1 1/3 tablespoon strawberry liqueur
- 7/8 cup sweet cream
- 1/8 cup sugar
- 1 package vanilla sugar
- 1/4 cup bittersweet chocolate frosting mix
- 2 teaspoons confectioners sugar for dusting

*Recipe is for 12 servings

Crème Brulee with Marinated *Strawberries*

Preparation:

1. Preheat oven to 250°F.

2. Cut open the vanilla pod lengthwise and remove the pulp. Bring the vanilla, milk, cream, and coffee beans to a boil.

3. In a second pot, mix the eggs with the egg yolk and 1 ounces of sugar. While stirring, add the milk mixture until the crème binds lightly. Pour through a fine sieve and divide among four flat ceramic dishes.

4. Cook the crème in the oven about 20 minutes. Take out, cover with newspaper, and let cool.

5. Wash and clean the strawberries. Puree 1/3 of them with the orange liqueur and honey; cut the rest into slices.

6. Wash the lemon mint, shake dry, and cut one sprig fine. Mix with the strawberry slices and puree and keep very cold.

7. To serve, scatter the remaining sugar on the crème and caramelize very quickly with a burner. Serve with the marinated strawberries and decorate each with a twig of lemon mint.

TIP: Any Number of Possibilities ... The relationship between crème and milk can be varied—the crème tastes very good even with milk alone. French chefs sometimes replace part of the crème with thin sour cream, giving the recipe a fresh, slightly sour flavor.

For the Crème Brulee:

- 1/2 vanilla bean pod
- 1 1/4 cups milk
- 7/8 cup sweet cream
- 1 tablespoon espresso coffee beans
- 3 eggs
- 2 egg yolks
- 1/4 cup sugar

For the Strawberries:

- 1/2 lb strawberries
- 1 tablespoon orange liqueur
- 1 tablespoon honey
- 5 sprigs lemon mint

Strawberry Carrot Cake

Preparation:

1. Preheat oven to 350°F.

2. Peel the French carrots, grate them fine, and let them drip-dry in a hair sieve. Mix the egg yolks to a foam with sugar, beet syrup, lemon juice, and zest, and fold in the French carrots. Sift the flour and the baking powder, mix with the almonds, and fold in the French carrots.

3. Put the dough in a 10-inch spring form lined with baking paper and bake golden brown in the oven about 35 to 40 minutes. Let it cool on a grid.

4. Wash and clean the strawberries, halve or quarter depending on size, and spread on the surface of the cake. Stir the frosting with the sugar and 1 cup of water according to the directions on the package, and pour it over the strawberries.

5. Roast the almond slices briefly in a coated pan without fat. Caution... they burn fast!

6. Stir the frosting smooth, warm it a little, coat the rim of the cake with it, and press on the almond chunks. Let the frosting become completely firm in a cool place. Decorate the cake with marzipan carrots.

For the Dough:

- 2/3 lb French carrots
- 5 egg yolks
- 3/4 cup sugar
- 2-3 tablespoons beet syrup
- Juice and zest of one untreated lemon
- 1 1/2 cups flour
- 2 teaspoons baking powder
- 2 1/3 cup ground almonds

For the Topping:

- 1 1/8 lbs strawberries
- 1 package cake frosting
- 1 tablespoon sugar

For the Decoration:

- 1/2 cup sliced almonds
- 2-3 teaspoons strawberry jam
- Small marzipan carrots

*Recipe is for 16 servings

Strawberry Punch

Ingredients

· 5 tablespoons caramel syrup
· 1/2 cup lemon juice
· 2 untreated oranges
· 2 untreated limes
· 1/2 lb strawberries
· Mineral water

Preparation:

1. Stir the syrup well with 1 1/2 cups water and the lemon juice, and pour into a punch bowl.

2. Wash the oranges and limes in hot water, rub thoroughly dry, and cut into thin slices or small pieces. Pour into the bowl with the oranges and limes and chill for about one to one and a half hours.

3. Before serving, fill the bowl with well-chilled mineral water and pour in glasses.

Strawberry Chili Drink

Ingredients

- 3/4 lb strawberries
- 1 cup skim milk
- 1 tablespoon chopped fresh mint
- 1 teaspoon chopped red chili pepper
- 1/8 cup oat bran flakes
- 1 teaspoon bittersweet chocolate sprinkles
- Fresh mint leaves

Preparation:

1. Wash and clean the strawberries and puree them with the milk.

2. Stir in the mint, chili pepper, and oat flakes.

3. Divide among glasses and spray with the chocolate sprinkles. Decorate with a few mint leaves.

Strawberry Margarita

Ingredients

- 1 2/3 lbs strawberries
- 2/3 cup white tequila
- 6 tablespoons confectioners sugar
- Juice of one lemon
- 12 tablespoons crushed ice

*Recipe is for 6 glasses

Preparation:

1. Wash and clean the strawberries. Save three berries for decoration. Puree the rest with tequila, confectioners sugar, and lemon juice.

2. Divide the ice among three glasses, pour in the strawberry margarita, and decorate with the remaining strawberries.

Strawberry and Semolina Flummery in a Glass

For the Sauce:

- 1/2 lb strawberries
- 3 tablespoons strawberry jam
- 2 tablespoons confectioners sugar
- 2 sheets white gelatin

For the Strawberry Salad:

- 1/2 lb strawberries
- 2 tablespoons confectioners sugar

For the Flummery:

- 3 1/8 cups milk
- 1/2 cup sugar
- 1 package vanilla sugar
- 1 pinch salt
- Grated zest of one untreated lemon
- 7/8 cup soft wheat semolina
- 3 large eggs
- 1/2 cup orange juice

*Recipe is for 6, 10-ounce glasses

Preparation:

1. For the sauce, wash and clean the strawberries and puree them with the jam and the confectioners sugar. Soften and dissolve the gelatin in cold water according to the directions on the package. Stir about 3 tablespoons of the sauce into the gelatin. Then stir the gelatin into the rest of the sauce.

2. For the salad, wash, clean, and slice the strawberries and marinate with the confectioners sugar.

3. Boil the milk with the sugar, vanilla sugar, salt, and lemon zest. Scatter in the semolina and cook for one minute while stirring. Take off the stove, cover, and let it settle for 5 minutes.

4. Separate the eggs and beat the egg whites stiff. Stir the orange juice into the egg yolks and fold into the semolina. Carefully fold in the egg white.

5. Rinse six glasses in cold water and put 2 to 3 tablespoons of semolina in each. Make alternate layers of strawberry salad, sauce, and semolina, finishing with a layer of semolina.

Strawberry Meringue Cake

Preparation:

1. Preheat oven to 400°F.

2. For the dough, stir the butter, 2/3 cup sugar, and the vanilla sugar to a cream. Separate the eggs and fold in the egg yolks one at a time. Sift the flour with the baking powder and mix with the oatmeal. Stir in with the milk.

3. Grease two, 10-inch spring forms and scatter oatmeal on them. Put half the dough in each form and bake for 10 minutes.

4. For the meringue, beat the egg whites stiff and gradually fold in the rest of the sugar. Spread half of the meringue on the warm bottoms of the cakes and bake 15 minutes at 325°F. Then bake another 45 minutes at 250°F and let cool.

5. For the filling, wash, clean, and slice the strawberries. Cover one cake with the strawberry slices.

6. Mix the cottage cheese, marscapone, sugar, and vanilla sugar and spread on the fruit. Put the second cake on top of it and chill for an hour.

7. Shortly before serving, sprinkle the cake with confectioners sugar.

For the Cake:

· 1/2 cup butter
· 1 3/4 cups sugar
· 1 package vanilla sugar
· 4 medium eggs
· 3/4 cup wheat flour
· 2 teaspoons baking powder
· 2/3 cup instant oatmeal flakes
· 6 tablespoons whole milk

For the Filling:

· 1 1/8 lbs strawberries
· 1 2/3 cup cottage cheese
· 1 1/2 cup marscapone
· 1/3 cup sugar
· 1 package vanilla sugar

Other Ingredients

· Grease for the forms
· Instant oatmeal for the forms
· Confectioners sugar

*Recipe is for 16 servings

TIP: Be Well Prepared... It is best to bake the cakes a day before; then it has just the right firmness for covering.

Index

Photo and Text Credits

I thank the following firms for their support:

- Almond Board of California
- Aurora
- Fish Information Center (FIZ), Hamburg
- Ketchum GmbH, Munich
- Bergader Private Cheese Shop
- State Union of the Bavarian Milk Industry
- Maggi Cooking Studio
- Peter Koelln KGaA, Elmshorn
- The Food Professionals Koehnen AG, Sprockhoevel
- Goldpuder
- Grafschafter
- Henglein
- Nutella
- Original Wein's
- Ostmann
- Ruegenwalder
- Toppits
- Wirths PR GmbH, Fischach
- www.1000rezepte.de
- Zott Allgaeutaler
- All other photos: Sammueller Kreativ GmbH